Presented to

_____

From

_____

A GIFT OF

Heaven

for Every

Heart

Stories for the Heart *Mini* Books

COMPILED *by* ALICE GRAY

Multnomah Gifts™
Multnomah®Publishers Sisters, Oregon

A Gift of Heaven for Every Heart
a Stories for the Heart *Mini* Book

© 2002 by Multnomah Publishers, Inc.
published by Multnomah Gifts™, a division of Multnomah® Publishers, Inc.
P.O. Box 1720, Sisters, Oregon 97759

ISBN 1-59052-024-6

Designed by Koechel Peterson & Associates, Minneapolis, Minnesota

Multnomah Publishers, Inc., has made every effort
to trace the ownership of all poems and quotes.
In the event of a question arising from the use of a poem or quote,
we regret any error made and will be pleased to make the
necessary correction in future editions of this book.

Please see the acknowledgments at the back of the book
for complete attributions for this material.

Scripture quotations are taken from *The Holy Bible*,
New International Version © 1973, 1984 by International Bible Society,
used by permission of Zondervan Publishing House;
The Holy Bible, New King James Version (NKJV) © 1984 by Thomas Nelson, Inc.

Multnomah is a trademark of Multnomah Publishers, Inc.,
and is registered in the U.S. Patent and Trademark Office.
The colophon is a trademark of Multnomah Publishers, Inc.

Printed in China

02 03 04 05 06 07 08 — 10 9 8 7 6 5 4 3 2 1 0

www.multnomahgifts.com

TABLE OF CONTENTS

Reference Point

Max Lucado

One of the reference points of London is the Charing Cross. It is near the geographical center of the city and serves as a navigational tool for those confused by the streets.

A little girl was lost in the great city. A policeman found her. Between sobs and tears, she explained she didn't know her way home. He asked her if she knew her address. She didn't. He asked her phone number; she didn't know that either. But when he asked her what she knew, suddenly her face lit up.

"I know the Cross," she said. "Show me the Cross and I can find my way home from there."

Jesus said, "Let the little children come to me, and do not hinder them, for the kingdom of heaven belongs to such as these."

MATTHEW 19:14

The heart longs for *heaven*,

heaven longs for the *heart*.

KIMBER ANNIE ENGSTROM

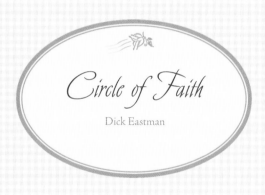

Circle of Faith

Dick Eastman

*L*ittle ten-year-old Maria lived in a rural village in central Chile. When her mother died, Maria became the "woman of the house," caring for her father, who worked the night shift at the local mine. Maria cooked and cleaned and made sure her father's lunch was ready when he left the house for work each evening.

Maria loved her father and was worried by how despondent he had become since her mother's death. Maria went to church on Sundays and tried to get her father to go with her, but he refused. His heart was too empty.

One evening, as Maria was packing her

father's lunchbox, she slipped a gospel booklet inside that she had received from a missionary worker who had been distributing them home to home in the area where they lived. Maria prayed that her father would read the booklet and find the comfort she had found in God's great love.

It was 1:10 A.M. when Maria was suddenly awakened by a horrible sound—the emergency whistle at the mine was blaring through the darkness, calling the townspeople to come running with shovels and willing hands to help dig for miners caught in a cave-in.

Maria made her way through the streets to

the mine in search of her father. Scores of men were frantically pulling debris away from the collapsed tunnel where eight men were trapped. One of the men was Maria's father.

Emergency crews worked through the night and finally broke through to a small cavern where they found the miners. Sadly, they were too late. All eight men had suffocated.

The rescue workers were devastated, but as they surveyed the scene, they noticed that the men had died, seated in a circle. As the workers looked closer they discovered Maria's father was sitting with a small gospel booklet in his lap opened to the last page where the plan of salvation was clearly explained. On that page, Maria's father had written a special message to his daughter:

My darling Maria,

When you read this, I will be with your mother in heaven. I read this little book; then I read it several times to the men while we waited to be rescued. Our hope is fading for this life, but not for the next. We did as the book told us and prayed, asking Jesus into our hearts. I love you very much, Maria, and one day soon, we will all be together in heaven.

The word *goodbye*

will never be used

inside heaven's gate.

The word *welcome*

will forever take its place.

JUDY GORDON

Heaven

Author unknown

Think of—

    Stepping on shore, and finding it Heaven!

    Of taking hold of a hand, and finding it God's hand.

    Of breathing a new air, and finding it celestial air.

    Of feeling invigorated, and finding it immortality.

    Of passing from storm to tempest to an unbroken calm.

    Of waking up, and finding it Home.

Coming Home

Sheila Walsh

I love homecomings. That's one of the reasons I treasure every opportunity I have to take a trip back to my native Scotland. On one such trip I was a guest singer at a Billy Graham crusade. I sat with the rain bouncing off the platform as George Beverly Shea sang the lovely hymn:

"Softly and tenderly Jesus is calling, calling for you and for me."

I looked out at the crowd gathered in a Scottish soccer stadium on that soggy Saturday afternoon and marveled that Dr. Billy Graham could fill the place. If it had been Chicago or New York, I would have expected a vast sea of faces, but there, on my own home ground, I was overwhelmed. I watched the crowd hanging on every word.

"Come home, come home
All who are weary come home."

Billy's message was simple and uncompromising. No bells or whistles "wowed" the crowd; just a simple call was made to "Come home." I looked out at shaved heads and tattoos, children running through umbrellas, and I wondered what the response would be.

I wondered if the message sounded too good to be true. I wondered if it sounded too simple.

But then it began… Like a waterfall, people began to stream to the front to receive Christ. I had to bury my face in my hands, overwhelmed with pure joy at being a spectator to such a homecoming. I thought of the Scripture, "I tell you that in the same way there will be more rejoicing in heaven over one sinner who repents than over ninety-nine righteous persons who do not need to repent" (Luke 15:7). I knew a big

homecoming celebration was going on in heaven right then.

When the crusade was over, I was waiting at the side of the stage for my ride back to the hotel. A woman wrapped in a plaid raincoat touched my arm. "I enjoyed hearing you sing tonight," she said.

"Thanks!" I replied. "Wasn't it a wonderful evening?"

"It was for me," she said. "I'll never be the same again."

"What do you mean?" I asked.

She stopped and looked at me for a

moment as if struggling to put it into words. "I've gone to church all my life, but tonight, I came home."

I put my arms around her and hugged her, and the tears and rain ran rivers down our faces.

Someone Is Waiting

Author unknown

John Todd was born in Rutledge, Vermont, into a family of several children. They later moved to the village of Killingsworth back in the early 1880s. There, at a very early age, both of John's parents died. One dear and loving aunt said she would take little John. The aunt sent a horse and servant, Caesar, to get John, who was only six at this time. On the way back this endearing conversation took place.

John: Will she be there?
Caesar: Oh, yes, she'll be there waiting up for you.

John: Will I like living with her?

Caesar: My son, you fall into good hands.

John: Will she love me?

Caesar: Aye, she has a big heart.

John: Will I have my own room? Will she let me have a puppy?

Caesar: She's got everything all set, son. I think she has some surprises, John.

John: Do you think she'll go to bed before we get there?

Caesar: Oh, no! She'll be sure to wait up for you. You'll see when we get out of these woods. You'll see her candle in the window.

Sure enough, as they neared the house, John saw a candle in the window and his aunt standing in the doorway. As he shyly approached the porch, she reached down, kissed him, and said, "Welcome home!"

John Todd grew up in his aunt's home and later became a great minister. She was mother to him. She gave him a second home.

Years later his aunt wrote to tell John of her own impending death because of failing health. She wondered what would become of her.

This is what John Todd wrote in reply:

Years ago, I left a house of death, not

knowing where I was to go, whether anyone cared, whether it was the end of me. The ride was long, but the servant encouraged me. Finally I arrived to your embrace and a new home. I was expected; I felt safe. You did it all for me.

Now it's your turn to go. I'm writing to let you know, someone is waiting up, your room is all ready, the light is on, the door is open, and you're expected! I know. I once saw God standing in your doorway... long ago!

"I go to prepare a place for you.
And if I go and prepare
a place for you,
I will come again
and receive you to Myself;
that where I am,
there you may be also."

JOHN 14:2–3, NKJV

Keep This for Me

"Keep this for me."

What child has not said this,

And placed a treasure in his mother's hand

With strict injunction she should keep it safe

Till he return?

He knows with her it will be safe;

No troubled thought or anxious fear besets his mind.

And off he runs lighthearted to his play.

If children can so trust, why cannot we,

And place our treasures, too, in God's safe hand;

Our hopes, ambitions, needs, and those we love,

Just see them, in His all-embracing care,

And say with joyous heart,

"Keep these for me."

AUTHOR UNKNOWN

Only Glimpses

Alice Gray

Laurel knew she was dying. Over the weeks, we talked often about heaven—what it would look like and how it would be to live there. It seemed we always ended up crying, and then holding each other tight.

The hardest part was trying to imagine something we had never seen, something about which we knew only a little.

And then I remembered this story....

The young girl with soft blond hair and eyes the color of sapphire had been blind since birth. Shortly after her twelfth birthday, a new technology was developed, and for the first time her doctor was hopeful that she would be able to see. Several months later, surgery was performed but the bandages could not be removed for two days. Until then, the outcome would be unknown.

The hospital staff brought a small cot into the girl's room so her mother could stay with her through the night. In the darkest hours, the daughter whispered, "Mother, are you awake?"

"Yes, dear, I'm awake."

"Mother, will you tell me again what it will be like when I can see?"

Reaching out in the darkened room, the mother found her daughter's hand. She stroked it softly as she described every lovely thing she could imagine.

Finally the moment came when the bandages

were removed. With sobs of joy the young girl saw her mother's gentle face for the first time. She reached up and brushed the tear from her mother's cheek and then traced her finger around her mother's mouth and brow, just as she had done when she was blind. Slowly, with arms wrapped around each other, they crossed the room and looked out the window.

Outside, fluffy white clouds sailed across a sky of faultless blue. Soft breezes stirred the cherry trees, and lacy blossoms sprinkled to the ground like pink snow. Yellow crocuses stood proud along the brick walkway, and a raspberry colored finch fluttered to the edge of a birdbath.

Wonder filling her eyes, the girl turned to her

mother.

"Oh, Mother," she whispered, "I never knew it would be so beautiful."

Tears filled my own eyes as I finished the story. I reached for Laurel's hand, not knowing what to say next. It was Laurel who spoke first.

"Right now," she said slowly, "I'm like that young girl in the story—waiting in the darkness, wondering what heaven will look like. Before long…I'll be seeing it for real. And with eyes filled with wonder, I'll turn to God and whisper, 'Oh, God, I never knew it would be so *beautiful.'"*

All the *goodness*

and *joy* and *warmth*

of the best of earthly homes

give us only an inkling

of our incomparable

home in heaven.

JULIA PENN

The Bells Are Ringing

James Dobson

A nurse with whom I worked, Gracie Schaeffler, had taken care of a five-year-old lad during the latter days of his life. He was dying of lung cancer....

This little boy had a Christian mother who loved him and stayed by his side through the long ordeal. She cradled him on her lap and talked softly about the Lord. Instinctively, the woman was preparing her son for the final hours to come. Gracie told me that she entered his room one day as death approached, and she heard this lad talking about hearing bells ringing.

"The bells are ringing, Mommie," he said. "I can hear them."

Gracie thought he was hallucinating because he was already slipping away. She left and returned a few minutes later and again heard him talking about hearing bells ring.

The nurse said to his mother, "I'm sure you know your baby is hearing things that aren't there. He is hallucinating because of the sickness."

The mother pulled her son closer to her chest, smiled, and said, "No, Mrs. Schaeffler. He is not hallucinating. I told him when he was frightened—when he couldn't breathe—if he would listen carefully, he could hear the bells of heaven ringing for him. That is what he's been talking about all day.

That precious child died on his mother's lap later that evening, and he was still talking about the bells of heaven when the angels came to take him....

❦

"And he will send his angels
with a loud trumpet call,
and they will gather his elect
from the four winds,
from one end of the heavens to the other."

MATTHEW 24:31

There is not a heart

but has its moment of longings,

yearning for something better,

nobler, holier than it knows now.

HENRY WARD BEECHER

Rejoice that your

names

are written in

heaven

LUKE 10:20

Springtime

Joseph Bayly

*O*ne Saturday morning in January, I saw the mail truck stop at our mailbox up on the road.

Without thinking, except that I wanted to get the mail, I ran out of the house and up to the road in my shirtsleeves. It was bitterly cold—the temperature was below zero—there was a brisk wind from the north, and the ground was covered with more than a foot of snow.

I opened the mailbox, pulled out the mail, and was about to make a mad dash for the house when I saw what was on the bottom,

under the letters: a Burpee seed catalog.

On the front were bright zinnias. I turned it over. On the back were huge tomatoes.

For a few moments I was oblivious to the cold, delivered from it. I leafed through the catalog, tasting corn and cucumbers, smelling roses. I saw the freshly plowed earth, smelled it, let it run through my fingers.

For those brief moments, I was living in the springtime and summer, winter past.

Then the cold penetrated to my bones and I ran back to the house.

When the door was closed behind me, and

I was getting warm again, I thought how my moments at the mailbox were like our experience as Christians.

We feel the cold, along with those who do not share our hope. The biting wind penetrates us as them....

But in our cold times, we have a seed catalog. We open it and smell the promised spring, eternal spring. And the first fruit that settles our hope is Jesus Christ, who was raised from death and cold earth to glory eternal.

We're Singing
Mother into Paradise

Helen Medeiros

I always remember the Twenty-third Psalm was my parents' favorite Scripture. Every night they would recite it together as they prayed for their eleven children and later many grandchildren and even great-grandchildren. After Dad died, Mom continued this tradition. We always knew we were loved and lovingly prayed for. It gave us comfort and even encouragement over the years. Then after Christmas a few years ago, we were called together once again when news came that Mom had another brain aneurysm. Fifteen years ago, she'd had a successful surgery on two other aneurysms, and we had been told there were several more. She could live two weeks or twenty years before another one might burst. So now, at the age of eighty-two, Mom lay in the hospital in Ottawa as the aneurysm began to slowly leak into her brain.

At first, she could communicate with us and indeed even talk and laugh at times, but as the leak grew worse, she became less and less coherent. We prayed with her, sang, and read Scriptures softly as she lay there. I had left my husband and four children in Bermuda to be with her, but as the days became weeks and Mom was still with us, I had to say my good-byes and go home to my family.

Knowing this would probably be the last time I would see my mother, I said my private farewells to her. By now her brain damage was so severe she could only speak a weak word now and then. Mom could no longer form a clear thought, let alone have any sort of con-versation. Indeed, she seemed to be slipping into a coma.

It was a cold snowy day in Ottawa, and I was alone with Mom in that hospital room. I hugged her and thanked her for her wonderful life. I thanked God for everything He had given us in her, and then I opened her Bible and began to read, "The LORD is my shepherd, I shall not want…." I finished the Psalm; she lay still and unresponsive. I then felt led to read it aloud to her again, this time saying, "Mom, the Lord is your shepherd, you shall not want; He makes you lie down in green pastures; He leads you by the still waters, Mom. He restores your soul…." I slowly finished with tears streaming down my face; then I turned and started to leave the room. Before I reached the door, I heard a clear, strong voice behind me, and I swung around. Mom was speaking with the voice of a young woman, "The LORD is my shepherd; I shall not want, He makes me to lie down in green pastures; He leads me beside the still waters, He restores my soul." I lifted my hands to praise Almighty God as she spoke every phrase with love, tenderness, and strength, finishing with, "And I will dwell in the house of the LORD forever."

With that last word, she lapsed back into semiconsciousness and never spoke another word. Two days later, the aneurysm burst, and the doctors gave her hours to live...but that mighty woman of God lived for another twelve days as we continued our vigil of thanksgiving, song, and prayer together. Always having been a musical family, we "sang our mother into paradise." As she took her last breath, we softly sang, "She is entering His gates with thanksgiving in her heart; she is entering His courts with praise."

The call of heaven

is the *sweetest music*

we will ever hear.

Its melody bids us to

"come home."

JUDY GORDON

Do You Know You're Going to Heaven?

The Lord Jesus has been preparing a special place in heaven—just for those who believe in Him. There will be no sickness, heartache, or tears. Instead, there will be peace and incredible joy.

Jesus said these very important words: "I tell you the truth, whoever hears my word and believes him who sent me has eternal life and will not be condemned; he has crossed over from death to life" (John 5:24).

Those who have received Jesus as Savior and Lord will be with Him in heaven through all the unending ages. Many years ago, I invited Jesus into my life with a simple prayer like this…

Dear Jesus, I believe that You are the Son of God, and that You gave Your life for me on the cross as payment for my sins. I believe that You rose from the dead and that You are alive today in heaven. Please forgive me for my sins and come into my life as Savior and Lord.

Thank You for the gift of eternal life. Help me to obey You and walk with You here on earth, until the day when I walk with You in heaven. Amen.

If you have sincerely asked Jesus into your life, He will never leave you. Nothing will be able to separate you from His love. And someday in heaven, on a bright eternal morning, we'll greet each other with a hug and laugh out loud for pure joy.

ALICE GRAY

Our home of

heaven is paved

with *welcome mats.*

JULIA PENN

Acknowledgments

"Reference Point" by Max Lucado, taken from *The Final Week of Jesus.* © 1994. Used by permission of Multnomah Publishers, Inc.

"Circle of Faith" by Dick Eastman, taken from August 1999 edition of *Every Home for Christ.* Used by permission.

"Coming Home" by Sheila Walsh, taken from *We Brake for Joy!* by Barbara E. Johnson, Patsy Clairmont, Luci Swindoll, Sheila Walsh, Marilyn Meberg, and Thelma Wells. © 1998 by Women of Faith, Inc. Used by permission of Zondervan.

"Only Glimpses" by Alice Gray. © 1999. Used by permission.

"The Bells Are Ringing" by James Dobson, taken from *When God Doesn't Make Sense.* © 1993 by Tyndale House Publishers, Inc. Used by permission. All rights reserved.

"Springtime" by Joseph Bayly. © 1973. Joseph Bayly, deceased, wrote a number of books including the apocalyptic novel, *Winterflight.* Used by permission.

"We're Singing Mother into Paradise" by Helen Medeiros. © 1999. Helen lives in Bermuda with her husband, four children, and four beautiful grandchildren. She is also a recent breast cancer survivor, thanks be to God Almighty.